PUERTO RICO
AND OTHER OUTLYING AREAS

by Jonatha A. Brown

GARETH**STEVENS**

PUBLISHING

A Member of the WRC Media Family of Companies

Please visit our web site at: www.garethstevens.com
For a free color catalog describing Gareth Stevens Publishing's
list of high-quality books and multimedia programs, call
1-800-542-2595 (USA) or 1-800-387-3178 (Canada).
Gareth Stevens Publishing's fax: (877) 542-2596.

Library of Congress Cataloging-in-Publication Data

Brown, Jonatha A.
    Puerto Rico and other outlying areas / Jonatha A. Brown.
       p. cm. — (Portraits of the states)
    Includes bibliographical references and index.
    ISBN-10: 0-8368-4674-5   ISBN-13: 978-0-8368-4674-4 (lib. bdg.)
    ISBN-10: 0-8368-4693-1   ISBN-13: 978-0-8368-4693-5 (softcover)
    1. Puerto Rico—Juvenile literature. 2. United States—Territories
and possessions—Juvenile literature. I. Title. II. Series.
    F1958.3.B76   2006
    972.95—dc22   2005044473

Updated edition reprinted in 2007. First published in 2006 by
Gareth Stevens Publishing
A Weekly Reader Company
1 Reader's Digest Rd.
Pleasantville, NY 10570-7000 USA

Copyright © 2006 by Gareth Stevens, Inc.

Editorial direction: Mark J. Sachner
Project manager: Jonatha A. Brown
Editor: Catherine Gardner
Art direction and design: Tammy West
Picture research: Diane Laska-Swanke
Indexer: Walter Kronenberg
Production: Jessica Morris and Robert Kraus

Picture credits: Cover, pp. 13, 22, 27 © John Elk III; pp. 4, 10, 16, 20, 23,
24 © Steve Simonsen; pp. 5, 15 © Eugene G. Schulz; pp. 6, 8 © North Wind
Picture Archives; p. 18 © James P. Rowan; p. 25 © Photo File/MLB Photos
via Getty Images

Printed in the United States of America

2 3 4 5 6 7 8 9 10 09 08 07

CONTENTS

Words that are defined in the Glossary appear
in **bold** the first time they are used in the text.

On the Cover: San Juan is a very old city. The oldest buildings date
from the 1500s. Today, the old and new lie side by side.

Introduction

If you could visit a tropical island, where would you go? Puerto Rico, perhaps? Puerto Rico has palm trees and sandy ocean beaches. The water along its coast is warm. People swim there all year long. The island has an interesting history, too. Spain owned this land for hundreds of years. It belongs to the United States now. Yet, in some ways, it is still more Spanish than American.

Clear waters lap a sandy beach in Boqueron, Puerto Rico.

The United States holds four other tropical island areas. The U.S. Virgin Islands are not far from Puerto Rico. The other areas are in the Pacific Ocean. They are American Samoa, the Northern Marianas, and Guam. Each island group is different, and each is lovely. They are all worth a visit!

The flag of Puerto Rico.

PUERTO RICO FACTS

- Became a Commonwealth: July 25, 1952
- Population (2007): 3,944,259
- Capital: San Juan
- Biggest Cities: San Juan, Bayamón, Ponce, Carolina
- Size: 3,425 square miles (8,871 square kilometers)
- Official Tree: Silk-cotton tree
- Official Flower: Puerto Rican hibiscus
- Official Bird: Stripe-headed tanager

History

Native people have lived in Puerto Rico for more than five thousand years. The first people were from South America. Some may have come from Florida. They lived mostly on fish. Later, many Natives grew crops and hunted birds for food, too. One of these groups was the Taíno. They grew sweet potatoes, corn, beans, and squash. Taíno women and men were equals. Women could be chiefs.

Another Native group, called the Carib, often attacked the Taíno. Usually, the Carib won these fights. The two groups were still at war when the Spanish first came to Puerto Rico.

The Spanish Come

In 1493, Christopher Columbus landed on the shores of Puerto Rico. He claimed the

In the 1500s, the Spanish forced the Taíno to be slaves. Many slaves worked in gold mines.

Changing Names

Christopher Columbus named the island when he claimed it for Spain. He called it San Juan Bautista. In Spanish, this name means "St. John the Baptist." When the Spanish set up a naval base in the city of San Juan, they called the city Puerto Rico. The name means "rich port." Soon, however, they changed the city's name to San Juan. The whole island became known as Puerto Rico.

island for Spain. Spanish settlers began to arrive in the early 1500s. The first group was led by Juan Ponce de León. They set up Caparra, a town on the coast. They found gold nearby. They captured the Taíno and made them slaves. The slaves worked in the gold mines.

Many Taíno died from diseases brought by the whites. Others tried to fight for their freedom in 1511, but the Spanish soon forced them back to work. Some of them ran away to live in the mountains.

The Spanish brought more slaves to Puerto Rico. These slaves came from Africa. Most of them worked in sugarcane fields on the island.

IN PUERTO RICO'S HISTORY

Creoles and Mestizos

The Spanish had many children in Puerto Rico. Sometimes, both of the parents were Spanish. Their children born in Puerto Rico were called **Creoles**. Other children were half Spanish and half Native American. They were **mestizos**. The Spanish and the Creoles had the most power and wealth. The mestizos had less. Slaves had no power at all and were very poor.

Controlling The Seas

Before long, all the gold was gone, yet Spain still wanted Puerto Rico. It began using the island as a base for its navy. This base was in San Juan. Soldiers and ships were stationed there. They helped Spain keep its hold on other islands nearby.

In 1898, the U.S. Army took control of Puerto Rico. Here, U.S. soldiers are shown arriving in Ponce.

In the late 1500s and early 1600s, both the British and the Dutch tried to take over Puerto Rico. They succeeded once or twice. Even so, the Spanish took the island back again.

Struggling to Survive

The people of Puerto Rico were allowed to trade only

IN PUERTO RICO'S HISTORY

Smugglers!

In the 1600s and early 1700s, most of the people in Puerto Rico were farmers. They were poor. Some began to sneak goods onto the island secretly. These people were **smuggling**. Smuggling helped them get the supplies they needed without paying taxes. When Spain let Puerto Rico trade with other islands, smuggling dropped off.

with Spain. They had to pay taxes on goods from Spain. Often they could not get the supplies they needed. The people of Puerto Rico grew poorer.

In the mid-1700s, Spain allowed Puerto Ricans to trade with people on other Caribbean islands. Early in the next century, Spain let the people have more say in their government. These changes did not last long. In the 1820s, Spain sent harsh governors to rule the island. A few of the rich people were in control again. They did little for the poor.

In the late 1800s, slavery was banned in Puerto Rico. A few years later, Spain gave Puerto Ricans more freedom to govern themselves. Once again, however, this freedom did not last.

IN PUERTO RICO'S HISTORY

El Grito de Lares

In the 1860s, some Puerto Ricans wanted to be free of Spain. Ramón Emeterio Betances was their leader. He wanted the people to fight for freedom. In 1868, his followers took over the town of Lares. They were no match for the Spanish. In just a few weeks, Spain was in control again. This short **uprising** was called *El Grito de Lares*, or "the Shout of Lares."

In 1898, Spain and the United States went to war. U.S. soldiers took over Puerto Rico. By the end of the year, they had beaten Spain. Now, Puerto Rico became a U.S. **territory**.

The United States used the island as a source of sugar and as a port for its navy. It built roads and schools. For most people in Puerto Rico, however, life was little better than it had

El Castillo San Felipe del Morro is a huge fortress in San Juan. It was built by the Spanish in 1539. Today, visitors can explore its secret dungeons and tunnels.

been. Many Puerto Ricans wanted to be free. In the 1930s, fighting broke out. Nineteen people died.

Change came slowly. In 1948, Puerto Ricans elected their first governor. They worked hard to solve their problems. Fewer people are poor today. Puerto Ricans are still trying to find the best way to work with the United States.

Famous People of Puerto Rico

Luis Muñoz Marín

Born: February 18, 1898, San Juan, Puerto Rico

Died: April 30, 1980, San Juan, Puerto Rico

Luis Muñoz Marín worked to help Puerto Rico become a commonwealth. He also became its first governor. When he was a young man, he had wanted the island to become a free country. By 1937, Marín had changed his mind, however. He started a political party that favored closer ties with the United States. Then, he was elected to the Puerto Rican Senate. In the Senate, he worked for more jobs, better schools, and improved health care. In 1948, the people of Puerto Rico voted for a governor for the first time ever. Marín won the election. He was reelected three times.

1493	Christopher Columbus reaches Puerto Rico and claims it for Spain.
1508	Juan Ponce de León and a group of settlers found the town of Caparra.
1518	Spanish ships bring the first African slaves to Puerto Rico.
1521	San Juan is founded.
1868	Puerto Ricans fight for freedom at Lares and are defeated.
1873	Slavery is outlawed.
1898	The U.S. government takes control of Puerto Rico.
1948	Puerto Ricans hold their first election for governor.
1952	Puerto Rico becomes a U.S. commonwealth.
1972	Roberto Clemente, a famous baseball player, dies in a plane crash.
1998	Hurricane Georges causes great damage.
2000	Sila Calderon becomes the first female governor of Puerto Rico.

People

Almost four million people live in Puerto Rico. More people live there than in many U.S. states. Most Puerto Ricans live in cities. About one-third of the **population** lives in or near the largest city, San Juan.

A Mix of People

Almost everyone in Puerto Rico has Spanish **ancestors**. They are Hispanic, or Latino, and they speak the Spanish language. About 80 percent of these people are white. Less than 10 percent

Hispanics: In the 2000 U.S. Census, 98.8 percent of the people in Puerto Rico called themselves Latino or Hispanic. Most of these people or their relatives grew up speaking Spanish. They may come from different racial backgrounds.

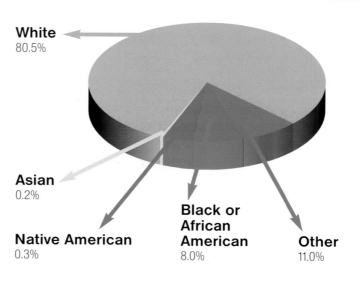

The People of Puerto Rico

Total Population 3,944,259

White
80.5%

Asian
0.2%

Native American
0.3%

Black or African American
8.0%

Other
11.0%

Percentages are based on the 2000 Census.

San Juan is on the north coast of Puerto Rico. Over five hundred years, it has grown to be the largest city in the commonwealth.

are black. Few people are Native Americans. Some of these people can trace their families back to the Taíno.

Not all of the early white settlers were from Spain. Some came from Germany, France, and Britain. In the 1900s, people moved from the United States to Puerto Rico. They added to the mix of people on the island.

Today, people still move to the island. Some are from the Dominican Republic. Others are from Columbia and Cuba.

Languages

Puerto Rico has two official languages. They are Spanish and English. About one in four people there speak both languages. Those who live in cities are more likely to speak English. Some people who live in the country speak only Spanish.

Religion

Long ago, the Taíno people believed in many gods and

goddesses. They called the gods and goddesses *cemis*. Some people still believe in cemis. They follow the old Taíno religion.

The Spanish brought the Catholic faith to the island. Over time, it became the main religion in Puerto Rico. Today, about three-fourths of the people are Catholic. Some people have mixed Catholic beliefs with those of other faiths. They have taken beliefs from the Taíno, African slaves, and other groups. Santeria is a mix of Catholic beliefs and African beliefs. Santeria came to the island from Cuba.

Most other people on the island are Protestant. A few are Jewish. Some people believe in spiritualism. They say that the spirits of the dead stay in our world.

Famous People of Puerto Rico

Rita Moreno

Born: December 11, 1931, Humacao, Puerto Rico

Rosita Dolores Alverio was born in Puerto Rico. Her parents were farmers. When she was five years old, she and her mother moved to New York City. She began singing on Broadway eight years later. She moved to Hollywood and changed her name to Rita Moreno. She grew up to become a very fine singer, dancer, and actress. Rita Moreno became the first person ever to win the highest awards in four areas. She won a Tony for performing in Broadway theater. She won an Emmy for acting on TV and an Oscar for acting in movies. She also won a Grammy for music.

Education

The earliest schools on the island were run by Catholic priests. Later, the Spanish government built schools in the cities. They mostly taught religion. At this time, books were rare, and few people could read and write. In the late 1800s, the Americans took over. They opened more public schools. Today, classes in public schools are taught in

Nearly every village and town has a Catholic church. This beautiful church stands in the town of Moca in western Puerto Rico.

the Spanish language. The children learn English, too.

Over half of all children go to college in Puerto Rico. It has about sixty-five colleges and universities. The biggest is the University of Puerto Rico. It is also the oldest. Its main **campus** is in San Juan.

The Land

Puerto Rico is smaller than most U.S. states. Only Delaware and Rhode Island have less land. Puerto Rico is made up of one big island and a few small ones. The big island is named Puerto Rico. Most of the small islands are off the east coast of this island.

Puerto Rico is about 1,000 miles (1,609 km) southeast of Florida. The Atlantic Ocean lies between them. The deepest spot in the Atlantic is not far from Puerto Rico. It is called the Puerto Rico **Trench**. The water is about 27,000 feet (8,200 meters) deep there. Another body of water lies off the south coast of Puerto Rico. This is the Caribbean Sea.

FUN FACTS

A Tropical Climate

Puerto Rico has a mild tropical climate. On most days, the temperature gets up to at least 78° Fahrenheit (26° Celsius) on the coast. Mountain areas are slightly cooler. The north coast gets much more rain than the south. Sometimes, hurricanes strike the island. The strong winds and rain can cause great damage.

A lovely green valley lies beneath the island's rugged hills.

PUERTO RICO

Mountains

Much of Puerto Rico is covered with hills and mountains. The big island has two mountain ranges. The Cordillera Central range is in the middle of the main island. It runs from east to west.

The highest peak in this range is Cerro de Punta. This peak is 4,390 feet (1,338 m) high.

Small rivers flow out of the Cordillera Central. The largest rivers flow north to the Atlantic. A few others flow south.

The other mountain range is the Sierra de Luquillo. It is in the northeastern part of the island. Between the two ranges is the Turabo Valley. Most of the land in this valley is used for farming.

Lowlands

A narrow strip of flat land runs along the north and south coasts. Most of the cities and towns on the island are located on this flat land.

In the northwest, the land is dotted with small hills. Limestone is the main kind of rock there. Rain has worn away the rock in some places to create caves and **sinkholes**. This type of land is called **karst**.

Major Rivers

Rio La Plata
46 miles (74 km)

Rio Grande de Añasco
40 miles (64 km)

Rio Grande de Loíza
40 miles (64 km)

La Coca Falls is just one of many amazing sights in El Yunque Rain Forest. This beautiful waterfall is 85 feet (26 m) high.

Plants and Animals

Tropical rain forests are found in the northern and central parts of the island. They cover mountains and hills there. Beautiful flowers bloom on some of the trees in the rain forests. Orchids and ferns grow in the rain forests, too. The Puerto Rican hibiscus is the official flower of Puerto Rico. It also grows in the north.

El Yunque is a big rain forest. It is in the Sierra de Luquilló. It gets 200 inches (5,080 millimeters) of rain each year. More than 240 kinds of trees grow there. Some of these trees do not grow anywhere else in the world.

Fewer plants grow in the south. Most are scrubby plants, and many have thorns. They are tough plants. They do not need much rain to grow.

Many kinds of birds live in Puerto Rico. Parrots, hummingbirds, pelicans, and herons are just a few of them. The stripe-headed tanager is the official bird. Big fish, such as tuna and marlin, swim off the coast.

The government of Puerto Rico has created a number of wildlife **preserves**. They protect the places where many birds, turtles, and other creatures live. They also protect trees that might otherwise be cut down.

Economy

Farming was once a way of life in Puerto Rico. This situation began to change in the 1950s. Today, far more people work in factories and other indoor jobs than on farms.

Goods and Services

Factories bring more money into Puerto Rico than any other kind of business. Some factories make medicines. Others make computer parts and tools used by scientists. Some make clothes.

Many people in Puerto Rico are **service workers**. Their jobs help, or serve, other people. Doctors, nurses, and teachers are

Millions of tourists visit Puerto Rico each year. Many come to the island on cruise ships.

service workers. **Tourism** also provides service jobs. Millions of visitors come to Puerto Rico each year. They eat in restaurants and stay in hotels. These places hire workers to help the tourists.

Many jobs are connected to the government. The U.S. Navy has a base in Puerto Rico. A U.S. Coast Guard training camp is there, too. These bases provide jobs for many people on the island.

Farming

Some people in Puerto Rico still work on farms. They raise cows, chickens, and pigs. Milk products bring in more money than any other farm product. Chickens and eggs rank second. Coffee and fruits are the leading farm crops.

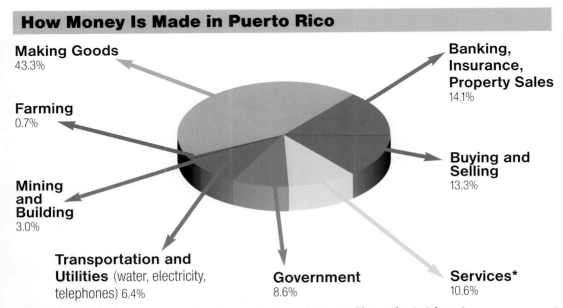

How Money Is Made in Puerto Rico

Making Goods
43.3%

Farming
0.7%

Mining and Building
3.0%

Banking, Insurance, Property Sales
14.1%

Buying and Selling
13.3%

Transportation and Utilities (water, electricity, telephones) 6.4%

Government
8.6%

Services*
10.6%

* Services include jobs in hotels, restaurants, auto repair, medicine, teaching, and entertainment.

CHAPTER 6

Government

Puerto Rico may seem like another country, but it is not. It is also not a U.S. state. It is a U.S. commonwealth. It has its own government and laws. As with states, laws in Puerto Rico cannot go against the U.S. Constitution.

San Juan is the capital city. The leaders of the commonwealth work there. The government has three parts. They are the executive, legislative, and judicial branches.

Executive Branch

The executive branch carries out the laws of the commonwealth. The governor runs

The capitol building is known as El Capitolio. It was built in San Juan in 1929.

The governor's house is a famous sight in Old San Juan. It was built as a fort in the 1500s.

this branch. Many other people help the governor.

Legislative Branch

The Puerto Rico legislature has two parts. These parts are the Senate and the House of Representatives. These two groups work together to make laws for the commonwealth.

Judicial Branch

Judges and courts make up the judicial branch. They may decide whether people who have been **accused of** committing crimes are guilty.

Local Government

Puerto Rico is made up of seventy-eight *municipos*. Municipos are like counties. Each one is run by a mayor and a group of people called an assembly.

PUERTO RICO'S GOVERNMENT

Executive		Legislative		Judicial	
Office	**Length of Term**	**Body**	**Length of Term**	**Court**	**Length of Term**
Governor	4 years	Senate		Supreme (7 justices)	To age 70
Secretary of State	Appointed by the governor	(27 members)	4 years	Circuit Court of Appeals (11 judges)	16 years
		House of Representatives			
		(51 members)	4 years		

23

Things to See and Do

Many people who visit Puerto Rico start in Old San Juan. The streets are paved with stones, and the buildings are very old. El Morro Fortress is nearby. The Spanish built this fort more than four hundred years ago.

Caguana Indian Ceremonial Park is also fun to visit. It has rock carvings that were made by the Taíno long ago. Taíno art can be seen at many museums, too. San Juan and Ponce have fine museums.

Festivals and Holidays

Puerto Ricans hold festivals all year long. The Ponce Carnival is held in the spring.

Rio Camuy Cave Park is near Arecibo. Here, you can explore parts of the third-largest cave system in the world!

Roberto Clemente became famous, but he never forgot the people of Puerto Rico.

Roberto Clemente

Born: August 18, 1934, Carolina, Puerto Rico

Died: December 31, 1972, between San Juan and Nicaragua

Roberto Clemente was a great baseball player. He played for the Pittsburgh Pirates for seventeen years. He won many awards for hitting and fielding. Clemente returned to Puerto Rico whenever he could. There, he coached children who hoped to become great ball players, too. He was a hero to many people in Puerto Rico. He died in a plane crash as he was helping bring food to people in Nicaragua after an earthquake.

A parade, dancing, and masks make this festival fun for all. San Germán hosts a Sugar Cane Festival. It lasts for a week and has music, dancing, and great food. Music and art festivals abound, as well.

San Juan Bautista Day is June 24. It honors the name Christopher Columbus gave the island. Discovery Day is a holiday, too. It takes place on November 19. This was the day Columbus first found Puerto Rico.

Other Outlying Areas

American Samoa

American Samoa is a U.S. territory. It is in the southern Pacific Ocean. It is a group of seven islands. The U.S. Navy took control of Tutuila in 1900. Over the next few years, it took over the other six islands.

Many people make a living by fishing for tuna. Others work in factories that pack fish into cans. Some people work in tourism or grow vegetables, nuts, and fruit.

Most people are **Polynesian**. They trace their families back to other South Pacific islands. A few whites and Asians live in Samoa, too. The people speak English and Samoan.

AMERICAN SAMOA FACTS

- Became a U.S. Territory: February 16, 1900
- Population (2007): 57,663
- Capital: Pago Pago (on Tutuila)
- Biggest Counties: Tualauta, Ma'oputasi, Lealataua, Ituau
- Size: 77 square miles (199 square km)
- Official Flower: Paogo
- Official Plant: Ava, also called kava
- Place to Visit: Fagatele Bay is a great place to see tropical fish.

NORTHERN MARIANA ISLANDS FACTS

- Became a U.S. Commonwealth: November 3, 1986
- Population (2007): 84,546
- Capital: Saipan
- Biggest Islands: Saipan, Tinian, Rota
- Size: 179 square miles (464 square km)
- Official Flower: Plumeria
- Official Bird: Mariana fruit dove
- Place to Visit: The American Memorial Park is on Saipan. It honors people who fought in a bloody battle there during World War II. The park is a nice place to jog, swim, and play tennis.

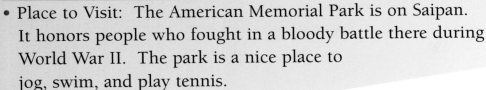

Commonwealth of the Northern Mariana Islands

The Northern Mariana Islands is a group of fourteen small islands. They are just north of Guam in the Pacific Ocean. They are part of a larger island group known as Micronesia. The United States took control of these islands during World War II.

Many tourists visit each year. They spend money at hotels and tourist spots. Tourism provides jobs for many workers. Some people grow fruits and vegetables. Some work in small factories.

Most of the people who live on these islands are Asian. They speak English and two Native languages. The languages are Chamorro and Carolinian.

Bird Island Lookout is a major feature on Saipan, the largest of the Northern Mariana islands.

Guam

Guam is an island in the western Pacific Ocean. It is in a group of islands called the Marianas.

The United States took control of Guam in 1898. It won the land in a war with Spain. U.S. military bases were built in Guam in the mid-1900s. Many people who live there work on these bases today. Others work in tourism or in the building **trades**. Some grow vegetables and fruits.

The first people to live in Guam were Pacific Islanders. Today, about half of the people are Pacific Islanders. Many Asians live in Guam, too. Most of the people speak English. They also speak a language known as Chamorro.

GUAM FACTS

- Became a U.S. Territory: December 10, 1898
- Population (2007): 173,456
- Capital: Hagatña
- Biggest Districts: Dededo, Yigo, Tamuning, Mangilao
- Size: 210 square miles (544 square km)
- Official Flower: Bougainvillea
- Official Bird: Mariana fruit dove
- Place to Visit: Cocos Island is a good place to swim and have a picnic. A Spanish ship sank nearby in the 1600s. Today, divers search the waters for treasure.

U.S. VIRGIN ISLANDS FACTS

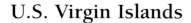

- Became a U.S. Territory: March 31, 1917
- Population (2007): 108,448
- Capital: Charlotte Amalie (on St. Thomas)
- Biggest Islands: St. Croix, St. Thomas, St. John
- Size: 134 square miles (347 square km)
- Official Flower: Yellow elder
- Official Bird: Yellow breast
- Place to Visit: Virgin Islands National Park covers more than half of St. John. It has thick rain forests and beautiful coral reefs. Visitors can hike and snorkel. They can see many interesting old buildings in the park, too. Another part of the park is on Hassell Island.

U.S. Virgin Islands

The U.S. Virgin Islands lie about 70 miles (113 km) east of Puerto Rico. More than fifty islands make up this group. Most are small. Denmark once owned the islands. The United States bought them in 1917.

Many people work in hotels and other places that serve tourists. Other people have jobs in factories. They make rum, cloth, and other goods. Some people have small farms where they grow vegetables.

Most of the people on the islands are African American or Hispanic. English is the official language. Some of the people speak Spanish and French. Creole is also spoken.

accused of — blamed for

ancestors — members of a family who lived long ago

campus — the place where a university or college is located

Creoles — Spanish people who were born in Puerto Rico or another colony of Spain

karst — an area made of limestone that has caves, holes, and underground streams

mestizos — people who are part Spanish and part Native American

Polynesian — from the South Pacific Ocean

population — the number of people living in a place, such as a city or state

preserves — places set aside to protect the plants and animals that live there

service workers — people whose job is to help or serve other people

sinkholes — holes in limestone where water collects

smuggling — bringing goods into a place secretly without following laws that apply to trade

territory — an area that belongs to a country

tourism — traveling for fun

trades — businesses that involve skilled work done by hand

trench — deep ditch

uprising — a fight by people against their rulers

Books

Puerto Rico. A to Z (series). Jeff Reynolds (Children's Press)

Puerto Rico. Festivals of the World (series). Erin Foley (Gareth Stevens)

Puerto Rico. Ticket to (series). JoAnn Milivojevic (Carolrhoda Books)

Roberto Clemente: Pride of the Pittsburgh Pirates. Jonah Winter (Atheneum/Anne Schwartz Books)

Web Sites

American Samoa National Park
syndication.getoutdoors.com/npca/destination_summary/5.html

Caribbean National Forest
gorp.away.com/gorp/resource/us_national_forest/
pr_carib.htm

Virgin Islands National Park
syndication.getoutdoors.com/npca/destination_summary/48.html

Welcome to Puerto Rico
welcome.topuertorico.org/

INDEX